Researcher
Jamie Wu Liu, M. A.

Content Editors
Kate Jack
Kim Van Gorp

Technology Editor
Jamie Wu Liu, M.A.

Project Manager
Paul Gardner

Editor-in-Chief
Sharon Coan, M.S. Ed.

Cover Designer
Lesley Palmer

Imaging
Ralph Olmedo, Jr.

Product Manager
Phil Garcia

Trademarks
QuickTime and the *QuickTime* Logo are trademarks used under license.

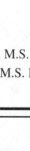

Publishers
Rachelle Cracchiolo, M.S. Ed.
Mary Dupuy Smith, M.S. Ed.

MULTIMEDIA
Collections
ELLIS ISLAND IMMIGRATION

Authors

Paul Gardner and Jamie Wu Liu

Teacher Created Materials, Inc.
6421 Industry Way
Westminster, CA 92683
www.teachercreated.com
ISBN-0-7439-3037-1
©2001 Teacher Created Materials, Inc.
Made in U.S.A.

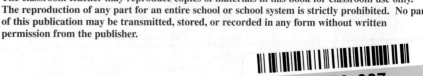

S0-BFA-337

Table of Contents

Introduction

The following guide is provided to assist teachers and students as they prepare to use the photographs, clip art, audio clips, video clips, and documents presented on the multimedia CD. The images and clips provide effective resources that teachers and students can use to enhance presentations and projects.

For your convenience, thumbnail images of the photos and clip art that appear on the multimedia CD are included at the end of this section. They can be viewed in advance to decide which images to use for a particular project or lesson. A list of the audio clips, documents, and video clips is also included.

Whether used for a student's written report or multimedia presentation, to enhance an instructional lesson, or to stimulate students' critical thinking, you will discover that the resource materials on the multimedia CD will help enrich your learning experiences.

Technical Support

Phone: 1-800-858-7339

Email: custserv@teachercreated.com

Web Address: http://www.teachercreated.com/support

Acknowledgments

HyperStudio® is a registered trademark of Knowledge Adventure.

Print Shop® is a registered trademark of Mattel Interactive.

System Requirements

Requirements for Macintosh

- 32 MB RAM

- PowerMac/100 MHz or faster

- System 8.0 or later

- Color Monitor (1000s colors)

- QuickTime 4.0 (or later)*

- 4X CD-ROM (or faster)

Requirements for Windows

- 32 MB RAM

- 486/100 MHz or faster

- Windows 95/Windows 98

- Color Monitor (High Color-16 bit)

- QuickTime 4.0 (or later)*

- 4X CD-ROM (or faster)

*QuickTime** is available on the CD-ROM or can be downloaded from: **http://www.apple.com/quicktime** See the ReadMe file for installation of *QuickTime* from the CD-ROM. Make sure you choose "Full" or "Recommended" as the installation type.

Getting Started

Since the program runs directly from the CD-ROM, there is nothing to install. However, if you use an older computer or have adequate disk space, it is recommended that you copy the entire CD-ROM onto your hard drive so that it will run more efficiently.

> **Macintosh Users:** In some cases, the viewer program will not work correctly with *Adobe Type Manager* installed on Macintosh. If you are unable to see media in the program, it is recommended that the **ATM** control panel be turned off. To do this, open the **Extensions Manager** in the **Control Panels** folder in the **Apple** menu. Uncheck the **ATM** control panel, save the settings, and restart the computer.

Follow these instructions to run the program directly from the CD-ROM.

Macintosh Users

1. Insert the CD-ROM into the drive.

2. When the CD icon appears on the desktop, double-click the CD-ROM to open it.

3. Double-click the Player icon to start the program (Figure 1).

Figure 1

Figure 2

Windows Users

1. Insert the CD-ROM into the drive.

2. If the CD screen (Figure 1) does not appear, click on the Start menu and then the Run menu (Figure 2).

3. Click the Browse button and locate the CD-ROM.

4. Locate the Player.exe file and double-click to start the program.

If you see a message that says "This program requires *QuickTime* version 4.0 or later…," you need to install *QuickTime*. Click on the QuickTime Installer on this CD-ROM, or download *QuickTime* from *http://www.apple.com/quicktime*

Follow these instructions to copy the CD-ROM onto your hard drive and run the program from the hard drive.

Macintosh Users

1. Drag the entire CD-ROM icon to your hard drive.

2. When the CD-ROM icon appears on your hard drive, double-click it to open the CD-ROM.

3. Double-click the Player icon to start the program.

Windows Users

1. Copy the contents of the CD-ROM into a folder on your hard drive.

2. Locate the Player.exe file and double-click to start the program.

Using the Viewer Program

The Main Menu

This is the menu that appears after the program is started.

Audio Clips
Click to browse only audio clips.

Clip Art
Click to browse only clip art.

Documents
Click to browse only documents.

Photographs
Click to browse only photographs.

Video Clips
Click to browse only video clips.

Desktop
Click to return to the desktop.

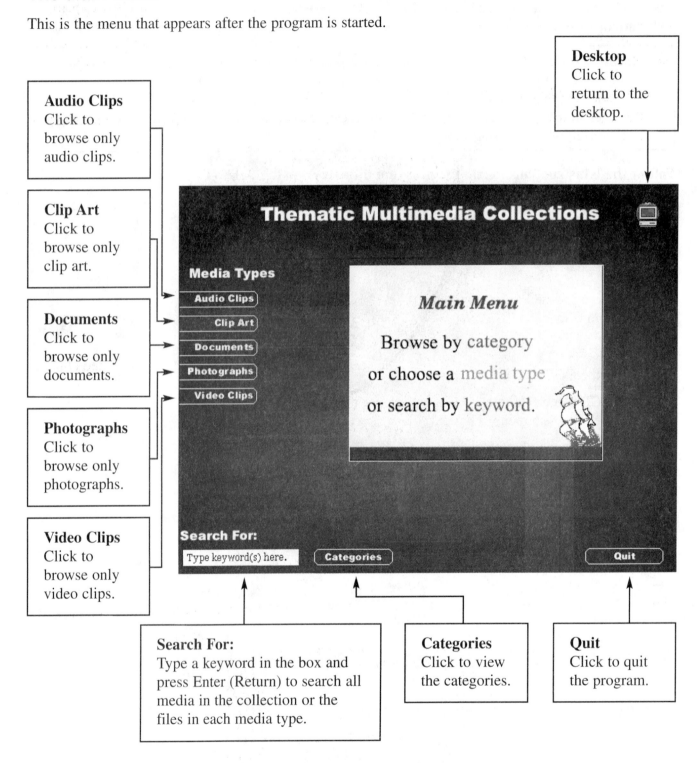

Search For:
Type a keyword in the box and press Enter (Return) to search all media in the collection or the files in each media type.

Categories
Click to view the categories.

Quit
Click to quit the program.

Using the Viewer Program

The viewer program provided on the multimedia CD allows the user to easily access the media by either browsing or searching with keywords. The user can choose a media type (audio clips, clip art, documents, photographs, or video clips) and browse the files in that media, or the user can choose a category and browse the files by categories. By entering a keyword(s) or the first few letters of a word, a search can be done to find specific files in all of the media types or in one particular media type.

Browsing by Media Type

1. Click a media type button (**Audio Clips, Clip Art, Documents, Photographs,** or **Video Clips**) to view the list of files in that media type.

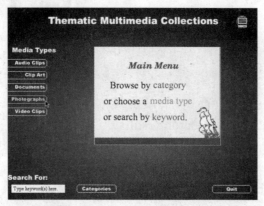

2. Click a file on the list to listen to the audio clip or look at the picture, document, or video clip.

3. Click the **Back to List** button to return to the list. Click the **Right Arrow** to listen to the next audio clip or view the next picture, document, or video clip. Click the **Left Arrow** to go back to the previous item on the list.

Searching by Keyword

The user can search in all media types.

1. Click on the **Main Menu** button to go to the main menu if you are not already there.

2. Type a keyword in the **Search For:** box and press **Enter (Return)** to view the list of search results. If no result is returned, try a different keyword. Typing in only the first few letters of a word gives the same result as when the entire word or a variation of this word is typed.

3. Click a file on the list to listen to the audio clip or look at the picture, document, or video clip.

4. Click the **Back to List** button to return to the list. Click the **Right Arrow** to listen to the next audio clip or view the next picture, document, or video clip. Click the **Left Arrow** to go back to the previous item on the list.

Searching by Keyword *(cont.)*

The user can also search in each media type.

1. Click the **Audio Clips** button.

2. Type a keyword in the **Search For:** box and press **Enter (Return).**

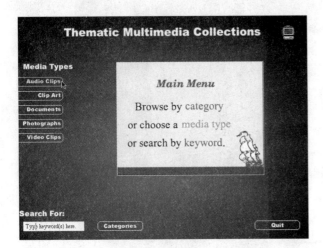

3. Click a file on the list of search results to select an audio clip (below left).

4. An audio control bar appears in the center of the screen (below right). Hold down the **Volume** key on the far left and scroll up or down to adjust the volume control. To listen to the audio clip, press the **Play** key (second from the left). Click on the **Rewind** key (second from the right) to rewind. The **Fast Forward** key is on the far right.

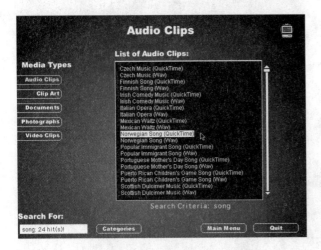

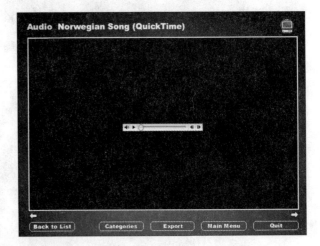

5. To search in another media type, click on the **Main Menu** button. Then, select that media type.

Using the Viewer Program

Browsing by Category

1. Click the **Categories** button to view the list of categories.

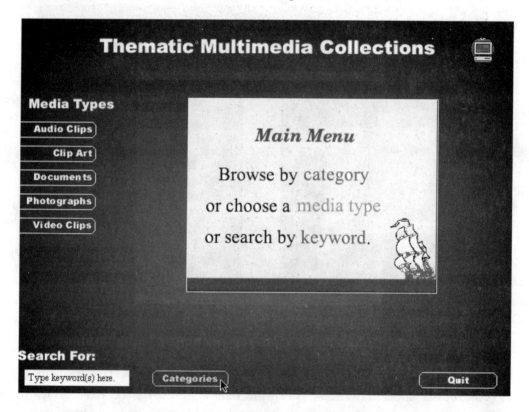

2. Click on a category title to view the files listed in that category.

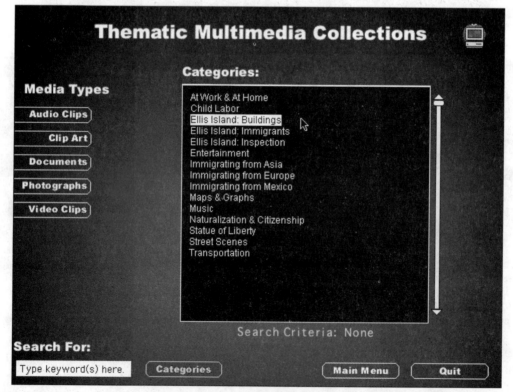

Browsing by Category *(cont.)*

3. Click a title to listen to the audio clip or look at the picture, document, or video clip.

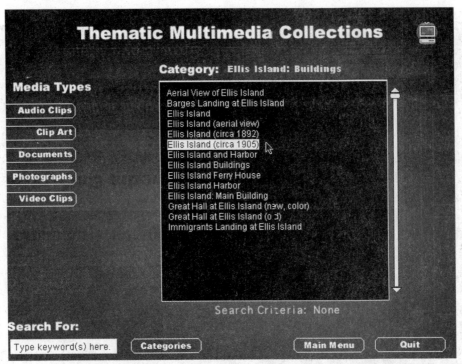

4. Click the **Back to List** button to return to the list. Click the **Right Arrow** to listen to the next audio clip or view the next picture, document, or video clip. Click the **Left Arrow** to go back to the previous item on the list.

5. Click the **Categories** button again and then click another category to view files in that category.

Copying and Pasting Photographs, Clip Art, and Text

The most efficient way to transfer photographs, clip art, and text from the viewer program into a document that you are working on is to copy and paste them. (*NOTE:* Audio and video files can be exported, but not copied and pasted; see pages 14 and 17.) Follow these easy steps to copy and paste.

1. Use the viewer to locate the photograph, clip art, or text that you want.
2. Click **Export** and choose **Copy to Clipboard**.

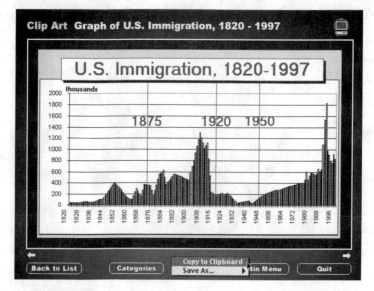

3. Click the **Desktop** button in the upper, right-hand corner to return to the computer's desktop.

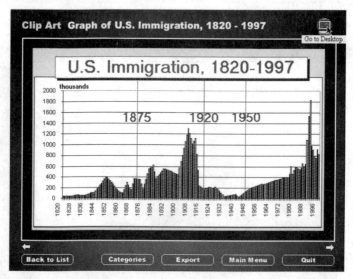

4. If you have not already done so, open the document in which you wish to add the media.
5. Choose **Paste** from the **Edit** menu in the application that you are using to create the document. To add more pictures, return to the viewer program and repeat the process. The viewer program continues to run in the background until you click **Quit**.

   NOTE: Some applications, such as *Microsoft PowerPoint*, require that you choose **Paste Special** from the **Edit** menu and then select the option Bitmap (BMP) or Picture (PICT).

Copying and Pasting Photographs, Clip Art, and Text *(cont.)*

The viewer program provided on the multimedia CD also allows the user to easily save photograph or clip art files to several popular file formats, including BMP, EPS, GIF, JPEG, PICT, and TIFF. Follow these instructions to export files.

1. Click **Export** and choose **Save As**...

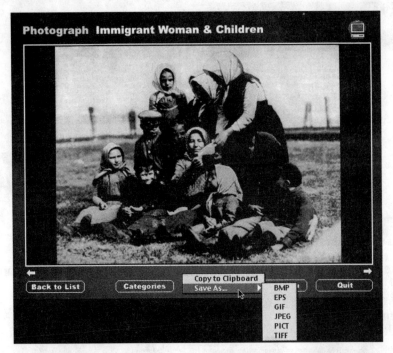

2. Choose the desired file format. (**GIF** export is not available on the Windows platform.)

3. Navigate to where you want to save the file (hard disk, floppy, etc.) and click **Save**.

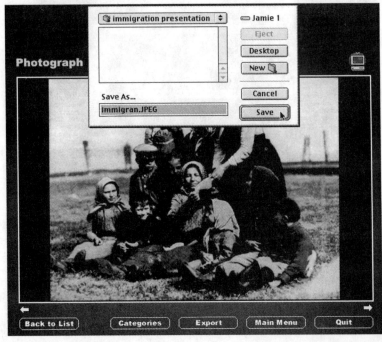

Listening to and Exporting Audio Clips

Media Types: Click the **Audio Clips** button to view the list of audio clips (music, sound effects, etc.). Click any of the audio files listed to listen to them. These files have been provided in two formats: QuickTime and Wav. Consult your software documentation to find out which format works best for your application.

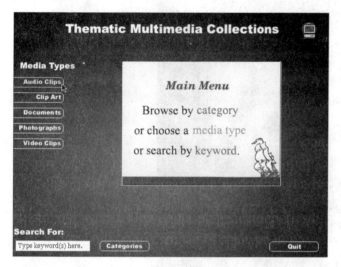
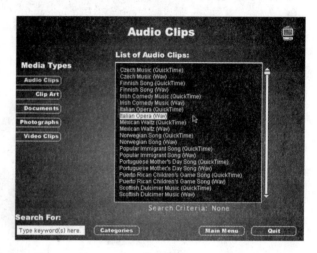

Search For: Type a keyword in the box here and press **Enter (Return)** to search only audio files.

Export: Click to export an audio clip for use in another program (see below). Navigate to where you want to save the file and click **Save**.

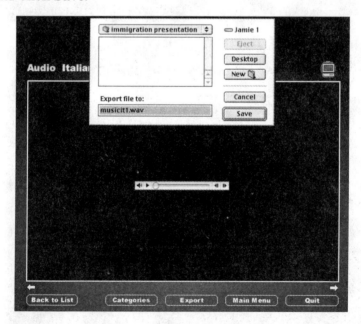

Back to List: Click to return to the list.

Arrows: Click the **Right Arrow** to go to the next audio clip and the **Left Arrow** to go to the previous one on the list.

Main Menu: Click to return to the main menu.

Viewing and Exporting Clip Art and Photographs

Media Types: Click the **Clip Art** or **Photographs** button to view the list of files. Click any of the clip art or photograph files listed to preview them.

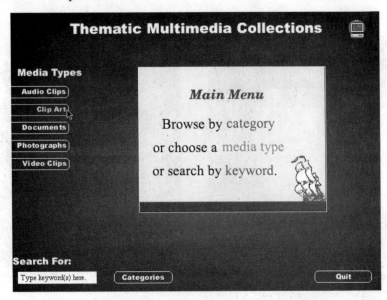

Search For: Type a keyword and press **Enter (Return)** to search only files in that media type.

Export: Click to export the image for use in another program. Choose **Copy to Clipboard** to copy and paste the image into another program, or choose **Save As...** and a file type to export the image for use in another program. (**GIF** export is not available on the Windows platform.) *NOTE:* Some applications, such as *Microsoft PowerPoint*, require that you choose **Paste Special** from the **Edit** menu and then select the option Bitmap (BMP) or Picture (PICT).

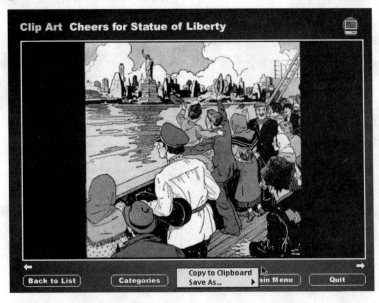

Back to List: Click to return to the list.

Arrows: Click the **Right Arrow** to see the next picture and the **Left Arrow** to go to the previous one on the list.

Main Menu: Click to return to the main menu.

Viewing and Exporting Documents

Media Types: Click the **Documents** button to view the list of documents. Click any of the files listed to preview the document.

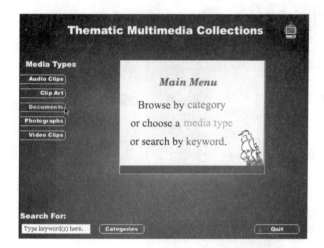
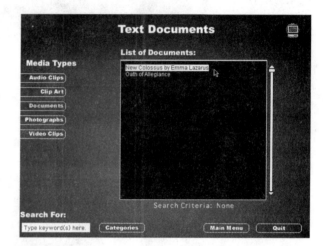

Search For: Type a keyword in the box and press **Enter (Return)** to search only the text documents.

Export: Click to export the text for use in another program. Choose **Export Text File** (below left) to copy the entire text of a document. Navigate to where you want to save the file and click **Save.**

Or, choose **Copy Selection to Clipboard** (below right) to copy and paste part of the text into another program. To select only part of the text, hold down the mouse button and highlight the desired text.

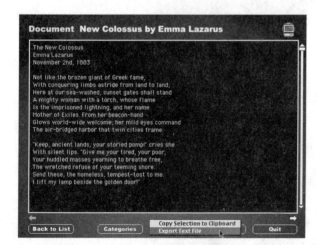
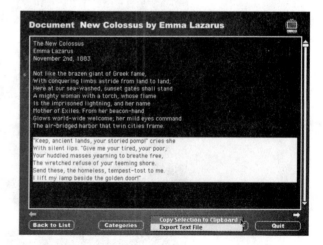

Back to List: Click to return to the list of documents.

Arrows: Click the **Right Arrow** to see the next document and the **Left Arrow** to go to the previous one on the list.

Main Menu: Click to return to the main menu.

Viewing and Exporting Video Clips

Media Types: Click the **Video Clips** button to view the list of video clips. Click any of the video files listed to preview them. Video clips are provided in both QuickTime and AVI formats. Consult your software documentation to find out which format works best for your application. On the Windows platform, AVIs are the most compatible with *PowerPoint*.

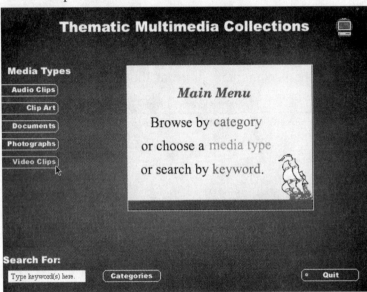

Search For: Type a keyword in the box and press **Enter (Return)** to search only video files.

Export: Click to export the video clip for use in another program. Navigate to where you want to save the file, and click **Save**.

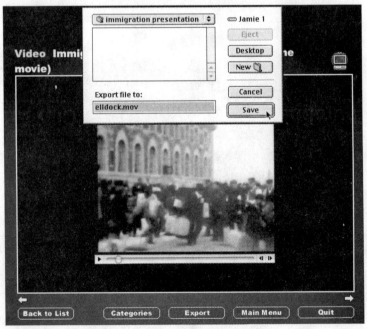

Back to List: Click to return to the list.

Arrows: Click the **Right Arrow** to see the next video and the **Left Arrow** to go to the previous one on the list.

Main Menu: Click to return to the main menu.

Ideas for Using Multimedia Collections in the Classroom

Teacher Uses

- Insert a series of photographs in a word-processing document and insert notes or captions. Print these on an overhead transparency and use them as visual aids.

- Use photos of people, places, and things as flashcards for students to study. For younger students, have them simply identify the photos. With older students, you can use the flashcards to have them identify the significance of the photographs.

- Import photos into a word-processing document to illustrate student work sheets. Have students explain the importance of the person, item, or event shown in the photos.

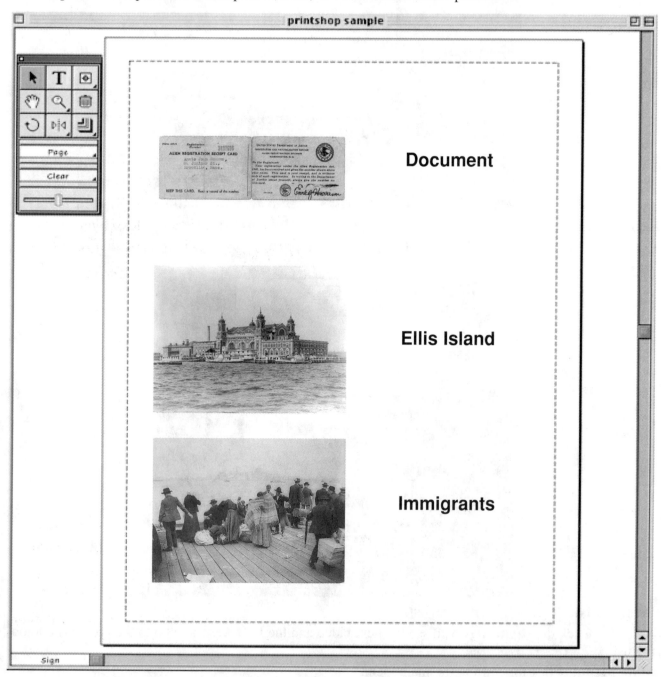

Ideas for Using Multimedia Collections in the Classroom

Teacher Uses *(cont.)*

- Create interactive practice activities using multimedia software such as *HyperStudio*.

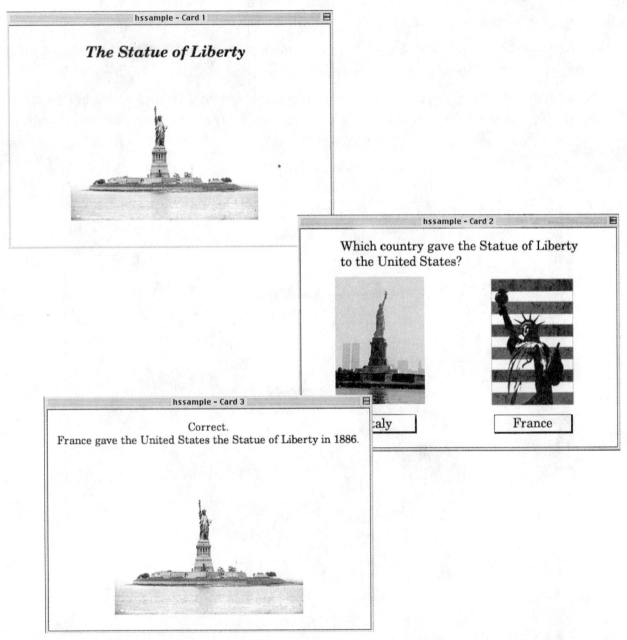

- Import a series of images into slide-show software such as *Microsoft PowerPoint*. Set the slide show to repeat itself on a computer at the front of the classroom or on a connected TV monitor. Use this simple slide show to grab students' attention as they walk into the classroom.

- Create a multimedia presentation using images and sound or video to illustrate your lesson.

- Make a Web page activity using the images and adding any hypertext links to sites you want your students to visit. Save the Web page to a folder on your hard drive so students can view it quickly. Include sounds or video clips to add more interest.

Ideas for Using Multimedia Collections in the Classroom

Teacher Uses *(cont.)*

- Open a video file in your Web browser for students to use at a learning center in your classroom. Provide students with several questions to answer about the images they see. You could also create a Web page with the questions and video file on one screen.

  NOTE: The HTML code for embedding a *QuickTime* movie file in a Web page is

  <embed src="file:///drive/folder/file" width="320" height="255" autoplay="true">

  where width is the width in pixels of the actual movie and height is the movie height plus about 15 pixels for the *QuickTime* bar at the bottom of the movie. The file location would be wherever you have saved it on your computer's hard drive.

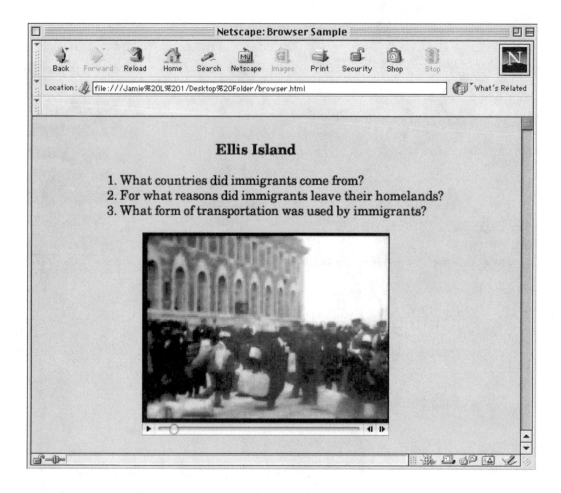

- Print a photo using word-processing or sign-making software, then use it as a bulletin board weekly challenge. Have a "suggestion box" under the photo and let students write their names and guesses on paper, then insert them in the box. Use that same image as part of a lesson once you have pulled all the entries out of the box. Award a monthly prize to the students with the most correct guesses. Create a certificate using all four of that month's challenge photos.

Ideas for Using Multimedia Collections in the Classroom

Student Uses

- Have students create diagrams by importing photos or clip art into a paint or draw program. Use the line and text tools to label parts or call attention to details.

- Students can import the images and other files into multimedia presentations rather than writing typical reports about the topic.

- Have students make posters about the people, places, and events of a particular time period. They can import a photo into word-processing or sign-making software such as *Microsoft® Works*, *AppleWorks* (formerly known as *ClarisWorks*), or *Print Shop*. Once they have researched the subject in the photo, they can create their posters and include important pieces of information.

- Students can make period newspapers. Have them use newsletter-making software or word-processing software to create newspapers for the time period they are studying. They can then import the photos or clip-art images to illustrate their articles.

- Let teams of students create challenges for each other. Have them use simple photo-editing software to add special effects to portraits of famous people in order to stump the opposing teams as they try to guess who the people are.

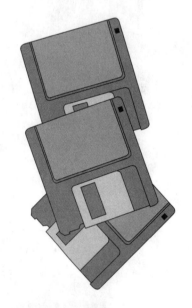

- Students can create multimedia presentations based on various songs included in the sound files. They can find the lyrics to the songs and use them as the headings on slides, adding photos that help illustrate the songs.

- Have student teams create multimedia presentations for a special technology parent night. Have them use the image, video, and sound files to create *HyperStudio* (or other multimedia program) presentations about what they have learned during their study of a particular topic. If you have a computer lab, have the students save their projects to various computers around the room. If you don't have a lab, try to get a projector or television connector so you can show the program to the entire classroom. Invite parents to come and have the students show off their presentations. You might want to invite the principal and board of education members to this event as well.

Student Uses *(cont.)*

- Students can write stories based on particular images. Have them import the images at the top of a word-processing document and then write about what is happening.

- Assign topics to the students and have them write research papers and import several images to help illustrate the topic. This is a great way to practice their word-processing skills.

- Have groups of students create multimedia presentations to "teach the class" about a concept you are studying. Each group in the class can have a different concept. They can use the image, sound, and video files in their multimedia presentations. You can keep these presentations on your classroom computer for students to use as review before tests.

- Have students create slide shows using *PowerPoint*, *HyperStudio*, or another multimedia program, adding their own narration rather than entering text into each slide. This may take some planning in order to find a quiet place in your room or a computer lab area for them to do the recording.

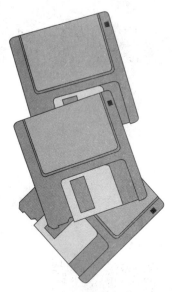

- Students could also present the "Morning News" in your classroom, using news clips from the time period you are studying. They could use the images and video files to represent the "filmed event" they are reporting. Videotape the students reporting the news with the computer monitor sitting behind them and facing toward the audience (and video camera).

- At the end of the year, have students create a multimedia presentation on "What We Learned This Year" to present to the next year's class. They could incorporate previous multimedia presentations or start from scratch and create a new project.

Thumbnail Photo Images and Clip Art

ellis9.jpg

Aerial View of Ellis Island

alcard.jpg

Alien Registration Receipt Card

flag.jpg

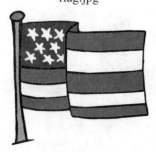

American Flag

angelis.jpg

Angel Island

angelarr.jpg

Angel Island: Arriving on the Pier

angel2.jpg

Angel Island: Buildings (color)

angel1.jpg

Angel Island: Immigration Station

citapp.jpg

Application for Citizenship, 1892

waiting4.jpg

Awaiting Inspection

barges.jpg

Barges Landing at Ellis Island

permit.jpg

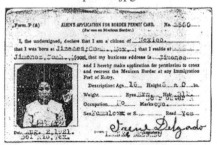

Border Permit Card

glass.jpg

Boy at Glass Works

boy.jpg

Boy Carrying Luggage

arrive.jpg

Carrying Luggage Off Boat

natcert.jpg

Certificate of Naturalization, 1916

stasight.jpg

Cheers for Statue of Liberty

twokids.jpg

Children at Ellis Island

ellis8.jpg

Children & Woman Waiting Behind Fence

chintown.jpg

China Town, New York

chinfam2.jpg

Chinese Family

manboy.jpg

Chinese Father & Son

chingirl.jpg

Chinese Girl & Older Boy

immship.jpg

Chinese Immigrants on a Ship

chinboy.jpg

Chinese Mother & Son

records.jpg

Clerks Studying Passenger Lists

landing2.jpg

Disembarking at Ellis Island

duchurch.jpg

Dutch Church

ellis.jpg

Ellis Island

elaerial.jpg

Ellis Island (aerial view)

ellis2.jpg

Ellis Island and Harbor

ellis5.jpg

Ellis Island Buildings

elis1892.jpg

Ellis Island (circa 1892)

elis1905.jpg

Ellis Island (circa 1905)

ellisfb.jpg

Ellis Island Ferry House

ellis6.jpg

Ellis Island Harbor

ellis4.jpg

Ellis Island Immigrants

mainbldg.jpg

Ellis Island: Main Building

athome2.jpg

European Man in Kitchen

europewm.jpg

European Woman Arriving at Ellis Island

extshop.jpg

Exterior of a Chinese Shop

pants.jpg

Family Making Pants

mideast.jpg

Family from Middle East

lettuce.jpg

Filipino Boys Cutting Lettuce

alienreg.jpg

Fingerprinting for Alien Registration

form.jpg

Form from the Department of Labor

frfisher.jpg

French Fisherman Bailing Boats

spin1.jpg

French Girl Spinner

shipger2.jpg

German Cruiser

Thumbnail Photo Images and Clip Art

graph.jpg

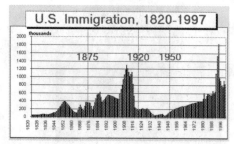

Graph of U.S. Immigration, 1820–1997

newhall.jpg

Great Hall at Ellis Island (new, color)

oldhall.jpg

Great Hall at Ellis Island (old)

family.jpg

Immigrant Family

yugoimmg.jpg

Immigrant from Yugoslavia

immigran.jpg

Immigrant Woman & Children

wagon.jpg

Immigrants at Battery Park, New York City
(circa 1900)

exameye2.jpg

Immigrants Being Examined 1

inspect2.jpg

Immigrants Being Examined 2

ellis3.jpg

Immigrants Landing at Ellis Island

dock1.jpg

Immigrants on Ellis Island Dock 1

dock2.jpg

Immigrants on Ellis Island Dock 2

Thumbnail Photo Images and Clip Art

ondeck4.jpg

Immigrants Resting on Deck

inspect1.jpg

Immigrants Waiting to Be Interviewed

officer.jpg

Immigrants with Officer at Gate

alone.jpg

Immigration Long Lines Cartoon

intervw.jpg

Immigration Officials Interviewing a
Chinese Man

immbldg.jpg

Inside the Immigrant Building

Thumbnail Photo Images and Clip Art

inspcrd.jpg

Inspection Card

intshop3.jpg

Interior of a Chinese Shop

irish.jpg

Irish Clam Diggers

bread.jpg

Italian Bread Peddlers, New York City
(circa 1900)

shipital.jpg

Italian Cruiser

field.jpg

Italian Field Workers

Thumbnail Photo Images and Clip Art

itbldgs.jpg

Italian Headquarters, New Orleans
(circa 1906)

mulst3.jpg

Italian Market

mulst4.jpg

Italian Neighborhood

mulst5.jpg

Italian Street Market

itstmrkt.jpg

Italian Street Vendor

itwork.jpg

Italian Women Picking Carrots

shipjap.jpg

Japanese Cruiser

jpcouple.jpg

Japanese Husband and Wife
(Identification Photos)

jpgarden.jpg

Japanese Tea Gardens

garters.jpg

Jewish Family Making Garters

jefarmer.jpg

Jewish Farmers

market.jpg

Jewish Market in New York City

jetemple.jpg

Jewish Temple

korean.jpg

Korean Gentlemen On Deck

appret.jpg

Labor Application for Return Certificate

liner.jpg

Large Crowd on Atlantic Liner

elgroup2.jpg

Large Group at Ellis Island

learn.jpg

Learning English

Thumbnail Photo Images and Clip Art

meximm4.jpg

Line of People at the Mexican Border

maps.jpg

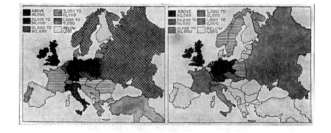

Map: Flow of Immigration

migratn.jpg

Map of American Immigration

irelamap.jpg

Map of Ireland

italymap.jpg

Map of Italy

ukmap.jpg

Map of United Kingdom

medexam.jpg

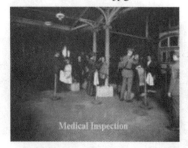

Medical Examination

athome3.jpg

Men & Children on Porch

meximm5.jpg

Mexicans at Immigration Station

mother1.jpg

Mother & Children on Ellis Island 1

mother2.jpg

Mother & Children on Ellis Island 2

mulst2.jpg

Mulberry Street Market

Thumbnail Photo Images and Clip Art

mulst.jpg

Mulberry Street, New York City
(circa 1900, color)

class21.jpg

Naturalization Class, 1921
(with only one woman)

natdoc.jpg

Naturalization Document, 1926

naturali.jpg

Naturalization in a New York Courthouse

newsboy.jpg

Newsboy

dock.jpg

Ocean Liner Unloading Immigrants

Thumbnail Photo Images and Clip Art

ondeck3.jpg

On Deck

ondeck2.jpg

On Deck (drawing)

ondeck1.jpg

On Deck (painting)

ellis7.jpg

On Ellis Island Dock

oyster.jpg

Oyster Shuckers

america.jpg

Patriotic Poster

Thumbnail Photo Images and Clip Art

waiting3.jpg

People in Inspection Line

spin2.jpg

Polish Boy Spinner

berry1.jpg

Polish Children Picking Berries 1

berry2.jpg

Polish Children Picking Berries 2

polish.jpg

Polish Immigrant Husking Corn

portuges.jpg

Portuguese Child in Field

rushouse.jpg

Russian House

russian.jpg

Russian Immigrants

sew.jpg

Sewing

mantags.jpg

Ship Manifest Tags

shrimp.jpg

Shrimp Picker

card.jpg

Statistical Card with Handwritten Notes

aerial.jpg

Statue of Liberty (aerial view)

statue2.jpg

Statue of Liberty (close up, color)

liberty1.jpg

Statue of Liberty
(close up, full length, color)

statimm2.jpg

Statue of Liberty & Immigrants
(from the shore)

statimm3.jpg

Statue of Liberty & Immigrants
(in background, color)

statimm1.jpg

Statue of Liberty & Immigrants (on ship deck)

Thumbnail Photo Images and Clip Art

liberty2.jpg

Statue of Liberty & Liberty Island

torch.jpg

Statue of Liberty Torch

statue1.jpg

Statue of Liberty with Flag Background

libsky.jpg

Statue of Liberty with Manhattan Skyline
(color)

harbor.jpg

Statue of Liberty with New York Harbor
(color)

nyimmigr.jpg

Street Crowded with Immigrants

Thumbnail Photo Images and Clip Art

swedish.jpg

Swedish Woman Arriving at Ellis Island

sweep.jpg

Sweepers & Mule Room Boys

oath2.jpg

Taking the Oath of Allegiance (group)

oath1.jpg

Taking the Oath of Allegiance (individuals)

flagstat.jpg

Torch and Flag

flagmap.jpg

U.S. Map with Flag Design

Thumbnail Photo Images and Clip Art

waiting2.jpg

Waiting on a Bench

exam.jpg

Woman at Examination

wmchild.jpg

Women and Children

elgroup1.jpg

Women at Ellis Island

women.jpg

Women Waiting with Children

worldmap.jpg

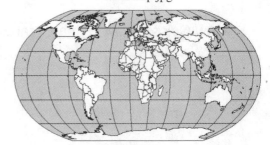

World Map

Audio Clips, Video Clips, and Documents

Audio Clips

Czech Music

Finnish Song

Irish Comedy Music

Italian Opera

Mexican Waltz

Norwegian Song

Popular Immigrant Song

Portuguese Mother's Day Song

Puerto Rican Children's Game Song

Scottish Dulcimer Music

Ship Taking Off

Spanish/Basques Song

Ukrainian Folk Song

Video Clips

Chinese Parade in San Francisco

Dancing: Japanese Women in Costume

Dancing: Spanish Gypsies

Ferryboat Landing at Ellis Island

Fish Market

Immigrants on Ellis Island Dock

Magician

Pushcart Vendors Selling Merchandise

View of the Statue of Liberty in 1898

Documents

New Colossus by Emma Lazarus

Oath of Allegiance